AF408193

MIKIYA WILSON

Colored By God: Black Girls Cry Too- A Black Girls Tale- With Poetic Prose

Black Girls Cry Too

First published by Mikiya Wilson 2024

Copyright © 2024 by Mikiya Wilson

All rights reserved. No part of this publication may be reproduced, stored or transmitted in any form or by any means, electronic, mechanical, photocopying, recording, scanning, or otherwise without written permission from the publisher. It is illegal to copy this book, post it to a website, or distribute it by any other means without permission.

First edition

This book was professionally typeset on Reedsy.
Find out more at reedsy.com

Contents

I Pray

1 The Truth:YOU HAVE LOST YOUR MIND   3
2 The Truth:YOU HAVE TO MOVE ON   9
3 The Truth: YOU HAVE A DYSFUNCTIONAL FAMILY DYNAMIC   12
4 The Truth:YOU HAVE ABANDONMENT ISSUES   14
5 The Truth:YOU HAVE BEEN TRAUMATIZED   17
6 The Truth:YOU HAVE BEEN USED BUT YOU CAN HEAL   21
7 The Truth:THE NARCISSIST DOESN'T FALL FAR FROM
   THE TREE   24
8 The Truth:YOU MARRIED YOUR FATHER   29
9 The Truth:SEX DOES NOT HEAL SEXUAL ABUSE   31
10 The Truth: YOU HAVE ANGER ISSUES   36
11 The Truth:IT'S A THIN LINE BETWEEN LOVE & CODEPENDENCY   39
12 The Truth:YOU HAVE TO FIND YOUR VOICE   43
13 Forsaking Yourself   47

II Forgive

III Deliverance

IV Renewal

V   Hope

VI   Grace

VII   Mercy

VIII   Faith

IX   Long-Suffering

14 Conclusion   67
Afterword   68

I

Pray

1

The Truth: YOU HAVE LOST YOUR MIND

Have you ever heard of the little saying ***"The truth will set you free?"*** Of course, you have. After attempting to resuscitate my failing marriage of ten years, heal from the pains of a narcissistic mother whose love and affection abated me, get the traumatic screams of my heroin addicted father out of my head, convincing myself that I too am a "WOMAN" after over ten years of infertility, running two-thousand miles away from the life I've ever known. It wasn't too long ago when I traipsed down the dark hallways of my house after I had been out drinking all night and thought it would be a great idea to tie a sheet around my neck and hang from the bathroom door. My naked body dangled from the door until the not so sturdy sheet I wedged in the top of it dropped me. There I lay, drunk, naked, and broken from the inside out, waiting for my alcoholic husband to find me and lift me up from the floor into his arms. Instead he lay in the bed hibernating from all the coke he shoved up his nose three nights earlier. Everything in my life was chaotic, and the dysfunction became the "norm."

The following morning, I picked my bruised body up from the bathroom floor and got ready for work. I remember sitting at my desk attempting to quiet the loud screams inside of my head. It's four-forty-five a.m. I am in a tiny caddy cornered cubicle next to a picture window, that looks out into one of the city's busiest highways. The city is over-populated, and the sounds of screeching tires, loud bangs, horns and sirens are a constant annoyance. I'd

3

like to find that peaceful place, that solitude that I love with deep passion. I'd like to go back to that hidden place that keeps me safe. Free from sound, free from people, free from it all. I sometimes imagine myself as being the only form of life remaining on a deserted island. I imagine the lonely seas without any living, creeping, crawling, swimming things. I am buried underneath myself. Covered under a blanket of false protection. I wear many masks day to day. I exist only to the small things. Yet, I find myself longing for the grandeur of things that bring forth great stories, events, seasons and times.

I feel a great presence that exists within. Yet I feel that it will take an eternity to find its true source. It is a feeling of running through dark deserts, rain forests, chasing an entity whose presence will not suffice. My soul cries out to God, in search of his face. I have lived carelessly, throughout the course of my life, and am now ready for instruction, reproof and rebirth. I am tormented day and night, with the overwhelming feeling of fear and failure. I am locked in a mental prison with bars that surround my carnal mind. I am like that of quicksand, sinking into the earth without an escape. My thoughts are not stable, and they toss me here and there, without a destination. I longed to taste the sweetness of this life and yet I have grinded into the depth of its bitterness instead. My imagination has run away with me, and I live in a world that is centered at the base of my mind. My dreams have abandoned me and turned me over to nightmares that await me in my sleep. I exist without a life that I love but have come to despise. I am running in slow motion, while all that surrounded me has trampled over all my small obstacles and have left me behind a thousand times.

God rescue me from these office walls that suffocate my soul and blind my life's vision. I need an escape from the mundane routine of Monday's and the turmoil of Tuesday's that lock me into a never ending cycle of UN-fulfillment and I sit quietly in this designated space with tiled ceilings and shades that never rise to avoid the glare on the computer monitors and in my spirit I feel a force that is wrestling with me and my strength has ran out before me and I am chasing after her: *"Come back, I cry out, but she does not hear my voice."* Instead she proceeds to run faster, stronger, harder, and I am left behind in a ball of weakness that seduces my inner man. In my dismay I continue to ask: *"Why God, am I moving at such a slow pace?"* "Why have my footsteps been tamed in such a manner that pulls me back from a great leap that I wish to take?" I am like that of the dust as from the beginning, when you formed me. Yet, endlessly seeking to be changed, knowing someday I will return to such.

I have spent countless years, walking around asleep. My body is alive in this earth, yet my inner being feels as though it has perished. What great foolish pride I've harnessed upon my back in my youthful years. A young girl, aimlessly seeking for love, attention and acceptance. What a foolish woman I've grown into, always thinking of the past and all its tragedies, triumphs, joys and pains. For once, I'd like to forget them all. I'd like to bury them under the sea of that deserted island I sometimes imagine myself living upon. I wish I could forget the sounds, smells, tastes and sights of all that I've ever known. I'd like to erase the memories, names, and faces. I am in despair as the constant scenes from my life replay over and over in the back of my mind. Why won't they let me forget, let me go, let me live, let me be free! I have been sleeping too long. Awake me to truth, sound judgment, faithfulness, and forgiveness. Bring me out of the dark trenches that hover over my life creating madness and deep confusion. It is you Lord who has kept, covered, protected, guided, and carried me. Even in the discontentment of my life and circumstances, you are a constant reminder of what I have escaped by grace.

Here I sit, in a half -furnished apartment, no children, no family, no laughter or jokes being shared while watching movies, or gathering at the table to share a meal. I relocated to a small town, two thousand miles away from my hometown to a city full of palm trees, mountains, and immense heat. I escaped the debris filled streets, the drug infested neighborhoods that were aligned with abandoned homes, empty lots, and buildings that were once great pinnacles of a fallen city. The corners filled with young black males waiting to be murdered on blocks they loved but did not love them back. I beat the odds of becoming a struggling single parent to children who I would have to raise up in poverty, and subject to a systematic society that sought to enslave them through the relentless grips of the ghetto. I lost the desire to get fixed up to go out to nightclubs, and after hour joints that stayed open to the wee hours of the night. A gathering place that housed men and women who enjoyed the late-night festivities and the company of familiar spirits that secretly danced with them in drunkenness, lustful filled eyes that gazed upon the faces and bodies of women who were dressed in sensuality, enticing the likes of men whose desires would carry them away.

I lost the desire to fix my makeup, glue hair extensions to my head, wear big clunky earrings, sit inside the Korean shop for a manicure and pedicure, where the screams of little kids unattended by their mom's would run around with bags of candy in their hands given to keep them content while their mother's spent a portion of their income tax money or their monthly cash benefit from their food stamp cards. drive around the neighborhood blasting the car stereo with my friends and crying drunk over our love lives. I grew tired of the late-night liquor store runs with drug addicts and drunks loitering and begging for change outside of them. I grew tired of drinking heavily to boost the confidence I needed to do things that my spirit rebuked Yet could not escape because of my lawlessness.

I tried to somehow fit in with people I have always felt different than, not because I was better, and they were worse, but because of the calling on my life that had separated me from the physical elements and exposed me to the great mystery of the spiritual. I had to escape from a life that cornered me into a system of complacency and government dependency. I felt a driving force calling me out from the works of the enemy that would attempt to use me where I was.

Finally, I became naked, and everything that my flesh has attempted to clothe with lies and deceit have been washed in his blood and I see the grime from the filth that once bathed me being washed away with every secret power that once controlled me and return unto the sewer from which it came. I was a high school dropout with no education and several failed GED attempts. I was receiving seven hundred and thirty-three dollars a month from social security and two hundred dollars in food stamps every month.

I was diagnosed with Poly-cystic Ovarian Syndrome (P.C.O.S) at the age of twenty-four. a hormonal imbalance that effects the endocrine system and causes infertility. I walked through the doors of the doctor's office with a million and one questions of why I had not been successful in becoming pregnant. *"You are not barren, you can have children, but you will need help getting pregnant."* Were the dreadful words that endlessly played in my head. I was saddened by the news and decided to ignore any necessary medical treatment to aid in the process of becoming a mother.

Eleven- years has passed since that time and I have a deeper longing to become a mother now, more than ever. Nonetheless, it was a blessing and a curse, because it prevented me from having children early on in my life, that undoubtedly would have been conceived with a man not suitable enough to be a father. Throughout the years it created in me a sense of worthlessness as a woman. I felt less than other women who were easily able to become pregnant, some of which included women I knew that were terrible mothers or who had no idea of who the father of their children were.

Moreover; I knew I was not ready to take on such a significant role in someone else life, due to the lack of opportunities that evaded me during those years, but my own selfishness for the things I thought could validate me as a woman kept the desire thriving, but the Lord's plans for me deterred me from certain burdens. I rented the upper flat of two-family unit in one of the city's most impoverished neighborhoods, riddled with crime and infested with heavy drug activity, home invasions, car jacking, rape and lewdness. The family that lived there before me, had completely ran the place down. It was infested with cockroaches, bed bugs, and even had mice.

I remember having an exterminator come out to the house, as he sprayed the top of the crown molding hundreds of roaches leaped and scattered from their hiding places, German cockroaches, big ones, medium ones and small ones. The bed bugs came out of their hiding places, they were so bad they were in the tile floors of the bathroom and came out when the floors were being replaced. They were in the walls, they came out of their hiding places in the living room when the exterminator sprayed, they were dehydrated without blood, and crawled slowly up the walls. The infestation of the cockroaches was so bad, I could smell the strong musty stench throughout the unit that would make you vomit. I could not eat inside of the unit for an entire month. I would have to eat my meals in my car, because the smell stayed in my nose and I would get nauseous at the thought of opening my mouth in that place.

I knew that I wanted and needed something more in my life. I was approved for "Section 8" subsidized housing assistance, but something went off inside of me and I envisioned myself being stuck in the vicious cycle of never truly being self-sufficient and relying on the seven hundred and thirty-three dollars check each month, and now I am approved for section 8. It was a test, and I had to decide for my life and my future. I knew that if I would have accepted the assistance, it would have hindered God's purpose for my life. I knew I had to put my trust in him and step out on faith and believe him to make a difference in my life. The decision did not come by way of my pride, it came through a breakthrough that I asked the Lord to make in me. I had to rebuke and bind the works of the enemy that wanted to keep me conditioned and low in spirit.

I had to make up in my mind that I was not disabled or incapable of providing for myself. I changed my thinking patterns, and I saw small changes in myself slowly begin to surface. I prayed and surrendered to God for deliverance to remove the weight of oppression from my shoulders.

I was a young woman in my late twenties, who unfortunately was not taught how to be self-sufficient in life. The world shaped me into who it wanted me to be. I had to break the cycle of dependency in my life that kept me unproductive, struggling, scheming and getting by, and that was only possible through the sacrifice of Jesus Christ. Only through his mercy, his love and grace. He called me out of the darkness of mental oppression. It did not happen overnight, but gradually, he picked away little things in my thought process and gave me a clearer prospective. I had to be re-introduced to spiritual thinking and concepts. Everything that the world taught and showed me was a smoke screen, lie and distraction. In some instances, I grew desensitized, because of the things I've seen.

At seven years old, I witnessed my uncle shot five times, in an alley. I witnessed my aunt as she was brutally stabbed in her back by her boyfriend. The world has a way of tainting you, exposing you, and contaminating you. It takes the cleansing through the blood of Jesus to remove the grit and residue from the world's programming.

2

The Truth:YOU HAVE TO MOVE ON

Once I made the decision to start a fresh new life and the painful choice to leave behind my family, and friends, I would soon grow tired of the social media accounts that were full of all kinds of spirits traveling through the connections of devices, transmitting ideas, beliefs, images and perceptions that invaded the internal minds of people.

We are sub-consciously emerged in a virtual world that makes a direct connection to our minds that give way to our spirits. Through controlled environments being used as a tool to produce heavy mind control by the gravitating force of this age that celebrates the world and the things in it. We have been conformed to this world and we blindly follow the leader. I am called to be awakened! Conscientious to the forces that lead us away for our lack of knowledge. A great deception that carries the people away as they sign up one by one feeding in to a system that gains spiritual access to everything about them through their most inner thoughts.

What struck me was a question one of the sites asked the people as they logged in. It wanted to know the thoughts of the people and the people did share. There was strife, desires, unhappiness, sadness, ridicule, cursing, explicit sexual content, anger, hatred, envy and sorrows that poured from the hearts of many. I watched as the lives of people unfolded, played out in a centralized scheme to track, monitor and manipulate the course of their lives through witchcraft, deep magic and spells.

All the while remaining hidden, nameless and faceless. What great deception exists that controls millions of people through the approach of social sites that are portrayed as an innocent means of connecting people to family and friends near and far, promote businesses etc. The craftiness of its true intent would bring forth great wealth for its creators to broaden its agenda. We are living among evil men who are in position to carry out the plans of the enemy, who comes to steal, kill and destroy.

There is a technological trance happening to the people, as they are sanctioned to virtual worlds filled with filth and lasciviousness. Come out from under the spells of this old ancient world and examine for yourselves the plot of things. Moreover: I found solace in the time I had alone and after filtering out all the things that unassumingly made me who I thought I was. I found that I did not know myself at all. Here I am at thirty-four years old, paying eleven- hundred dollars in rent, two hundred dollars in my bank account, one- hundred and seventy dollars on one of my high interest credit cards, and seventy dollars on the other. I wonder often what my life's purpose is, and when that purpose would come to fruition. I had to get uncomfortable with who I was, what I allowed in my life, and what I settled for. Everything that provoked a change in me, were the things that first had to make me uncomfortable.

God has a way of making you uncomfortable in situations, to bring you out of them. As of now, I will get ready for bed and set my alarm for four a.m. Get into my overpriced vehicle that I am financing and drive to my nine to five call center job. Log in for work, and place calls to patients who have not used their copay cards, or need to re-enroll for continued benefits. I will smile at all my co-workers and my boss who stands over my shoulder micro managing my every move.

I will even be nice and engage in meaningless small talk with the weird girl that creeps up behind me every day at work, to tell me stories about her last date with a guy she met on some random dating app, that only wanted to have sex with her, or about what kind of latte she drinks, and what the difference between a latte and a coffee is. I will listen to a bunch of frustrated coworkers with attitudes give program information to complaining and confused patients and pharmacies.

I'll continue with my daily routine of coming home to this one-bedroom apartment, that faces the parking lot. Right now, I only have a couch and TV, with no bed, because of the invasion of bed bugs into my brand-new king-size bed set. I will wait by the phone every evening at seven forty-five for a collect call from the prison. Eat junk food, sleep on the corner of my sectional couch that is beginning to sink in from my body weight on it every night and watch my fifty-inch TV that I scored from the pawn shop for one hundred dollars. All these things, I will do until I find a purpose to my unfulfilled life.

3

The Truth: YOU HAVE A DYSFUNCTIONAL FAMILY DYNAMIC

I am Mikiya. I was born August 8th, 1982 in Chicago, Illinois. I was the second child born to my mother Lena and my father James. I also have an older brother, James Jr. My parents were married and very much in love until my father's drug addiction fueled a life of instability both financially and mentally. Although my mother loved my father deeply, she could no longer bare the pain of being with a drug addict any longer. My parents separated and that was the first stage of failure for them and us a family. They eventually agreed on how the custody between the two of us would be divided. They decided the best solution was for my brother to stay with my dad, and I with my mother. After their marriage dissolved my mother went on to develop a new relationship with my stepfather Richie. They met at my mom and dad's wedding, Richie was the brother of the man who married my mom's best-friend Brenda. They were married the same day at the same venue. Years after my parent's separation they would reunite for a short time. Richie along with some of his friends would later be arrested in one of the suburbs of Chicago for robbing a liquor store. *"Now we are thrusted into the complex world of making a living without the head of provision in our lives, and now we go on without men who swore to protect, guide and shelter. Now we tread upon the serpents of an unjust system that seeks to tear us down with low paying jobs, public housing, and road blocks that create back routes and a gateway to destructive alternatives. Now we seek something, anything to numb the pain of our sufferings, now we create addictions, depression, abusers and the model book for failures. Now we begin to mimic those things that influence how we love, think, understand, commit and create conflict resolution. And now the blood of the innocent is lost in the things we did not teach.*

Now we seek God for the things we cannot control. Now we seek what is greater than ourselves, circumstances and trials. Now we learn to apply faith for the things we hope for, now we have birthed the need of an almighty God to do the work of men who were not worthy, now we desire to be embraced by him who does not disappoint nor abandon. Now we know we are powerless in this life we were given and now the seed is planted in us to rely not on ourselves, but an invisible source."

4

The Truth:YOU HAVE ABANDONMENT ISSUES

Everything in my life that was supposed to shield, nurture, mold and guide me had forsaken, ignored, and threw me to the wolves. I sought rest in my deep affliction, and I was a hopeless, lost wanderer seeking rest from my troubles. I can still feel the sadness that loomed in the air, a dark mist hovering over us during that time. I can still hear old R&B tunes playing throughout the house, telling stories of a woman's heartbreaks and pain through song. Those old records played, and I felt the connection between me and the power of penetrating words and it was a presence that danced with the lowly in spirit and the stories seduced a desire in me to be a woman before my time and the melodies strummed the wonder of my emotions, invoking sensuality in my young self. Over the years my mother struggled with her own addictions and mental health issues. One afternoon at her friend's house she attempted suicide. She was brought out on a stretcher and lifted into the ambulance to be taken to the nearest hospital. I heard as her best friend Brenda explained to the Emergency Technicians (EMT's) that she had taken a bottle of pills and tried to kill herself. My heart sunk at the news and I remember looking up at the trees watching the early bloom of the new leaves that began to grow. They were bright orange and yellow in color. The gravity of sadness swept me from the ground and carried me away, but the clouds would not provide me rest, they tossed me back down to the concrete and I was shattered into pieces by its cruel embrace. There I stood among many, yet alone. For many years the spirit of defeat followed me, like a shadow. A taunting reminder and instigator that I would someday meet a similar fate. It would be many years later, before I could go through that pain and search to see the things I could not see, listen for the things, I could not hear. It was a baggage claim process for me. I had to put myself in her shoes and connect with her pain before the healing could begin.I particularly felt the deep manifestation of the things and incidences in my life most profoundly take effect in my adolescent years. I had a deep desire to be approved by my peers and anyone that would take liking to me. Like many other young girls, I too was a victim of sexual abuse. I can still remember the feeling of hands that caressed me in the night and the stench of a pedophile that crept through my bedroom door.I felt an overwhelming feeling of being powerless, paralyzed and fearful. I began to mask my emotions and bottle them up inside. I would cut myself with knives to release the pain I was feeling. There was a sense of relief I felt when I would push the Knife deeper into my skin and the release it gave me. The spirit of destruction was upon me and had manipulated me into self-harm. I went into myself further and further and I hid all my truths deep inside my young self.Moreover; My mom's depression seemed to last for an eternity. It forced me to enter a state of solidarity, and seclusion. I developed mass insecurity as a young girl. I can remember being eleven years old and my mom being locked in her room with my younger brother, hiding herself from me and the rest of the world, like she had the Davinci code or some top-secret thing that could change the world or create a revolutionary event. I can remember the silence that filled the halls of the house, silent screams seeping through the walls, weeping quietness, that pierced my eardrums like scraping of nails against a chalk board. *"What have I done to you mother? What am I, that you cannot love? What clever device exists that could make you see me?!'* I imagine there are none. I was invincible to my mother's love. We lived our lives inside of that tiny duplex and communication eluded us. The only thing that separated us was the walls dividing the two rooms. I took refuge in my room and went into a world of my own, mastering the art of using my imagination as an escape.

And I went crazy in that house without any sound and the muted memories still spins endlessly paused records that never seem to playback whenever I recount.

5

The Truth: YOU HAVE BEEN TRAUMATIZED

My father would come around every so often or I would go to visit him at my grandmother's house where he lived. My visits to see my dad, were just as painful and traumatizing as the time spent with my mom. My father would lock himself in his room, where he would shoot up and go off into this dark universe. I sometimes wondered where that place was.

What was so great, and wonderful about that place, that you can go anytime you like and never be concerned with the life you hold a physical place in. As a young girl, I often flirted with the idea of using heroin. I fantasied about the needle piercing my veins and the rush of the heroin flowing through them as they did my father's. One night I stayed over my grandmothers with my brother and I heard screams and groaning from a belting man. Sounds of a man as if he was being stabbed a thousand times repeatedly. I discovered that no one was harming him at all, but my father was having severe heroin withdrawals, and he was in agonizing pain. I can still hear the awful screams. They were loud, and they were frightening sounds revealing to me the screams of a tortured soul lost in an earthly hell with death as a bed of rest.

I went into my father's room after he had fallen asleep and I slept in his arms shortly until my grandmother made me go back to my brother's room to sleep. I wanted to stay with my father throughout the night and my heart poured out letters that could not reach him in time:

*"Dear sweet father, what pains doth ye bear so deeply that arrest thee? How so have these webs entangled thee? Does thou knoweth not that ye are loved by a daughter who needs thee? For your eyes hold secrets that hide thee. Come out from under your sorrows and see the beauty of the stars that giveth light unto the dark skies. Smell the flowers that bloom in early May. For the sand of the earth awaits thy weary feet. Come father and seethe magnificent seas that provideth a home to the creatures both great and small.Hast thou not known mercies of the glorious one that has kept thee? He hast forsaken ye not my sweet father. For he awaiteth patiently to hear thou humble cry. I needeth thy hand, but for a moment, to lead thee into the lighted area, just there in the open foyer where the chandelier hangs adjacent to the living quarter. Has thou soul left out from amongst thee? Please returneth back to me my sweet father whom I love and adore.Expose now what great thing thou hast doneth that thou cannot evade. Are there no quiet seas that could calm thee? Whatever pains ye bear have been given to our heavenly father who hast canceled thy sins. Be not afraid for here ye are loved unconditionally as ye hast also loved. -***A letter to my father**

I would sometimes write these mellow dramatic poems, filled with mystery and passion. I consider it to be a great escape for the *"Brokenhearted."*

I learned early on through my father's battle with heroin addiction the powerful stronghold and oppression that drugs birth in the lives of people. I would sit and watch as my father sat in the floor high out of his mind from the effects of heroin flowing through his veins. He made weird sounds with his voice and spirits spoke out of his mouth, using his lips to speak coded languages that were not understood. He would snap his fingers against his head and demons used him as a puppet on a string.

This strong, gentle man, whom I loved and adored was absent, and bound by an unseen force controlling his mind and body. He was lost in darkness, trapped in the devil's paradise of torture and false fulfillment for a temporary fix, a high that would destroy his entire life and keep the shackles around his ankles until his demise. I cried for his life and I cried for his love. I would often attempt to brace myself for his death. I wanted him to be given rest from the misery that accompanied him. Each time we were called and asked to hurry to the hospital after he would overdose, was like driving a knife through my heart, a thousand times. Drug addiction is a powerful tool used by the enemy to house demons that have been given authority to use its hosts.

I knew then that the devil and his devices were real, and I experienced first -hand the devastating effects and damage he persistently projected in my father's life. I would enter my father's room and throw out his needles so that he could not shoot up. I found a syringe in the bathroom at three years old and pushed down the plunger and my father's contaminated blood spewed out.

I witnessed the hidden grips of bondage through the life that was stolen from my sweet, charismatic, strong, loving, and handsome father. All the things I looked forward to experiencing in my life with him, would NEVER come. They would pass us by, like that of a log drifting in the sea, never meeting the shorelines. I could feel the longing he had for someone to be there. One night while I was out with a friend of mine and asked her if we could make a stop along the way, so I could see me father. I went into my father's room and he was sobbing and greeted me with a hug. I held him tightly in my arms briefly, before sitting on the edge of his bed with him. I asked my father, *"What is wrong?"* He wept, as he pulled open his bathrobe to reveal his bare frail chest to me.

I looked to see what he had to show me, and he continued to cry while pointing to the huge mass that grew on his chest the size of an orange. He said: *"I don't know what's wrong with me."* His health was deteriorating, and the physical signs began to scare both he and I. I pulled him closer and held him in my arms and we cried together that night, like so many others. But unlike those times, this would be the last.

A few months later he overdosed and was admitted into the hospital. I went to visit him early one morning and was told of his passing the day of my visit. The pain toppled me over! All of the memories flashed before my eyes in that moment. What a sad way for a young girl to spend hers days. Worrying about a father who played Russian roulette with his life. Everyday of my life after that day, I wondered what he could have been or how our lives would be, if he hadn't ruined it all. I will never know. I had to bury his legacy of heartache, dysfunction and way of love. I had to learn that it's not okay to allow someone to subject you to their madness.

It's okay for YOU to be protected and nurtured with healthy love. Unfortunately, it took year after year after year for me to come into that realization. After all of the men, after all of the tears. I finally got it. I accepted being used and abused, because I was taught indirectly through the relationship with my father that pain accompany's love. I spent years in a vicious cycle of never being able to say no!

6

The Truth: YOU HAVE BEEN USED BUT YOU CAN HEAL

I returned home to my mother and things were as they were when I left. My brother James would come over to stay with us for a while. While he was staying with us, he had several boys from the neighborhood come over. I had sex with one of my brother's friends that my mom let come and stay with us. He and his twin brother Melvin stayed at our house because they were kicked out of their family's house.

One night while my mother was away at work, one of the twins Melvin asked me to come to the basement with him. I went to the basement with him and we begin to kiss and touch each other. Melvin was more advanced than me, and it was rumored that Melvin had a baby with a girl in another part of town, and that he was a deadbeat dad, who was not interested in having any kind of relationship with the child. I was eleven years old with no real understanding about what qualities to look for in a *"Man."* We continued to kiss in a moment of dry passion. In my hesitation, I stopped him as he proceeded pulling my pants off. I took my underwear off and inside was a blood-soaked bulky pad that lined them. I could feel the heavy flow of blood trickling down my thighs, staining the uncovered mattress that was in the center of the linoleum floor of the basement.

I can still hear the rumbles of the furnace coming from the dark wash room, and the cold chill that blew through the cracks of the small windows that brought a peak of moonlight that made the cobwebs covering the smudged glass visible. Unequivocally a virgin for a short time. Unaware of the seed of sexual immorality being planted. Afterwards, I went upstairs to my room and laid on my bed, confused and scared. Melvin comes upstairs to my room and asks if I am okay.I shook my head yes, but inside my eleven-year-old self quite unsure.

I had to look up to the heavens,
   just to be sure the sky ain't fall on me.
   I placed my broken brown body
   inside the cast iron tub and lit cinnamon
   scented candles all around,
   hoping it would
   relax the *"Dancing"* parts of me.
   I soaked hours
   tryna get that grit off me.
   I was all black and blue on the inside.
   I could feel my
   limbs trying to run away from me. They were all
   worn and tired of chasing after hopeless things
   for me. I had strikes from lightning that
   produced scars on me.
   All these hands on me! I never remembered if
   honey came out them suckles for me.
   I had to be free and ran out naked into the cold winter
   streets.
   I was cold like ice and all my woman
   parts froze on me.
   All these damn bodies on me!
   I rubbed myself down in turpentine covering
   my face, palms and all my limbs.
   The roars of thunder exploded the drums of my ears.

I was looking through the mirrors trying to find a shadow of me.
There were small shriveled up curls atop my head
after emerging from the water.
Suds dripping and watery eyes.
My mind seems to always run after thangs it just can't find.

Throughout the life of my sexual encounters, I noticed myself beginning to act like men I slept with.Particularly one who I had been intimate with on a consistent basis. I developed his language and mannerisms. I had this spirit of a man living inside of me from all the years I spent having Pre-marital sex with him. His spirit was embedded deep inside of me.

I could hear his voice when I spoke and there was a discerning spirit that would call me to confront that spirit that dwelled within me for years. I had a desire to come into God's calling, but I was being held back by this spirit that warred against my femininity and planted a seed of masculinity. I had to trace the events of my life and sought to uncover the cause. I needed to be the woman God created and not this *"Thing"* that changed my personality, language and spirit. I could feel the strings of my heart being tugged and the desire to be used by God would force me to identify the things in my life that was not of him.

I would be well in my mid-thirties before I finally sought deliverance from his spirit. The grips of sin can manifest itself in any dimension or aspect of your life, mind and body. I was constantly used by older boys in the neighborhood who could see me coming from a mile away. I spent a lot of time consumed by promiscuity as a teenage girl. I had a deep longing for a father who was absent and strung out on drugs. I hoped one day he would come and rescue me from all the boys and men that did not love me, but only wanted to use me and throw me away. I had a heart that yearned for my mother's affection. Yet could not find it.

7

The Truth: THE NARCISSIST DOESN'T FALL FAR FROM THE TREE

At the age of fourteen I inherited my mother's depression and developed her same isolation techniques. I mastered being alone as if it was my second nature. My mother gave me a book set that included chronicles of different fantasy worlds, unknowingly introducing to me the world of deep occultism and stories of magic, witches and secret passages to a magical land. I was completely enamored by this book and spiritually susceptible to hidden forces penetrating my very young and impressionable mind.

The stories fed my desire to be taken away to another place. It gave me an escape and pushed me further into a world of my own imagination. I begin to hear voices and see demonic spirits in my room at night. I could not sleep at night without hearing voices telling me they were in me. I was petrified by my reality. I would go into my mother's room at night to get in the bed with her and my younger brother because I could not sleep alone. I was living a complete nightmare, and I suffered during that time. One evening I went into the basement to wash laundry, and out of the pits of hell I heard vividly two voices arguing with each other right beside me!!

The nature of their conflict was not revealed to me in that moment and the language was unknown, as it was not English. I ran up the stairs fast like lightning, heart pounding, terrified and uncontrollably shaken! I had lost it. It was till this day the most terrifying and most prolific spiritual event of my life.I was introduced to the Lord at an early age and the lord gave me spiritual gifts that the physical world does not understand with spiritual eyes and ears, but that of the carnal mind. I noticed these attacks coming soon after I was saved and gave my life to Christ. The lord began to reveal the truth of who is to me. He revealed things to me that are of the spiritual realm. One day after reading my bible, I took a walk around the neighborhood, and the scales removed from my eyes. It was the first time I was able to see the world for what it truly is.

The dark principalities that ruled the air and the magnificence of light that existed in the heavens. It was God giving me the knowledge of good and evil. I would go on to live my life as freely as I chose, but never forgetting the seeds that the lord planted in me, never digging out the root of his word that was planted in me. I continued in my sin but began to have great convictions. The voices and visions became more than I believed I could bare.I attempted to kill myself by drinking an entire bottle of cough syrup. I thought that would for sure take me out of my misery and save me from the voices. I was afraid and called my aunt to tell her what I had done. I was having full on demonic attacks that only prayer and true deliverance could save me from. Over the next day or so, my mom admitted me into one of the local mental institutions.

I sobbed uncontrollably and wept as I entered the doors of this very real and scary place.I was fourteen years old and had to be admitted into a psyche ward for hearing voices. I settled in and became acquainted with other teenagers who had been admitted to the institution for different spiritual attacks that grappled their lives by way of mental illness. It was a powerful experience for me at that age. There were so many young teens in the mental ward for some of the same things I was battling. There were other teens admitted into the institution for everything from hearing voices, compulsive lying, hallucinations, depression and many other issues. I remember my mom brought a reverend to come and pray for me on one of her visits.

I remember his hands being placed over my head, and a prayer filled with holy ghost power that he spoke into my soul, rebuking illness, and the forces of the enemy that came to take my mind. Although my mother struggled in her life and bared her own pains of heartache and loss; I was grateful that she knew God and taught me about his greatness and his mercies. I admired my mother for her courage and strength to overcome demons in her own life. It will forever be with me, as sure as I live. During my stay at the ward, I was scheduled one or two visits with my Psychologist every other week or so. On this evening with my Psychologist during my initial evaluation. I expressed what I was experiencing and what lead to my admittance into the facility.

The doctor wanted to put me on "Psyche meds" to help with the voices. I refused and told the Doctor: *"I don't believe I need to be on medication."* He asked: *"Why don't you feel you need medication?"* I looked him in his eyes with his degrees and his knowledge of mental health, psychology and how he and so many other trained professionals spent years studying and examining the human nature of man, and deep inside my fourteen-year old self, through the knowledge of Christ and the wisdom he gave me at an early age.

I knew that I had to confront the spiritual and divine realm and not the physical. There was no answer, no help or deliverance that HE could give me. I replied with great enthusiasm, grounded and rooted in my faith and beliefs, and I said to him: *"I feel like what I'm going through is spiritual and that God and the Devil is fighting for my soul."* This revelation came to me by way of the demons that I encountered in my basement that night. At the time I did not understand the meaning or could not grasp the concept of exactly what was taking place. I was frightened and had to get out of there as soon as possible. I thank God for his mercy and grace in my life every day.

Taking medication was not an option for me.

I relied on the lord for my strength and deliverance, and he brought me out of the darkness that invaded my life. Otherwise, I would have been destroyed. I would have lost that of the natural mind if I relied on things created by man to somehow save me. Instead, I sought after the only source, healer and miracle worker who provides a way out of no way, who says yes when the world says no, he who listens intently when your cries, screams, fears, and insecurities go unheard by men.

There is an omnipotent God, a counselor who waits for the call. It would have been a never-ending battle without God. I would have been lost, stuck in a vicious cycle of doctors and medications to keep me protected from these spiritual forces in my life. Jesus was my answer for the hopelessness, insanity, and confusion that lurked in the corner of my heart and mind. God kept me and carried me through those trying times of my life, and I give all glory and honor to the creator of my soul.Throughout my teenage years, the lord would give me his word to hide deep in my heart, send angels to protect me, and send prophets to deliver revelations to me.

I was a young UN-witted soul when it came to the exploration phase of traveling and going to and from. I would often get lost or turned around, as my sense of direction was like that of blind mice going through a maze. One morning, I got ready to attend the new Preparatory school, after being expelled from the public-school system. I caught the bus as planned and got off the bus at the wrong exit. I walked through the streets of the city to find my way, when I came across a pay phone. I entered a quarter into the slot to place a call to my mother, and out of the side of one of the buildings across the street from the pay phone emerged a man who greeted me. He began to pray for me and asked me to bow my head. He from his lips started to reiterate prayers of mine from the night before, aloud. I can remember the feeling of being in a screenplay.

It was as if there was a "Lot" laid out for me that day, and the scene was set with fake buildings, people that passed by in the background, like that of movie extra's in a film and a single payphone as a prop and the bus was the vehicle that took me to that destination. It took me exactly where God had intended for me to be that day. While in prayer my mother picked up the other end of the phone, and I told her a man was praying for me and had introduced himself to me as a prophet. Rightfully reluctant, my mother advised me to get away from the man, as he could have been a nut case. However, I did not shew him.I felt a connection with him.

I believed him to be who he said he was. After he finished praying for me, he gave his name to me as Thomas and he said I would see him again. A few months later, I took my older cousin up on an offer to accompany her to one of the main Libraries in town. As I walked through the library, there at one of the small tables next to the back row of books sat a man whom I instantly recognized.I walked over to him and I said: *"Hi, do you remember me?"* He replied with a pleasant yes, and welcomed me to his table, and there I sat. He began to point out people in the library that had demons inside of them, they were strange looking people that had an eerie presence that filled that side of the library.

I looked up at each one of them as he pointed them out, they were standing there with their faces buried inside of books, women, men, black and white.One thing that stood out to me was the thick bifocals that were worn by one of the women Thomas identified as being filled with demons, and she looked up and around as if someone had spoken her name and her cover was blown. One by one, these individuals he identified, began to disperse and leave out of the library, it was in total to my recollection seven of them who exited from the building simultaneously.

Thomas went on to say that when the spirit of the lord is in a place, demons must flee, and they did. It was a divine moment in my life as God revealed to me the spiritual realm of demons that walk, live, gather and breed amongst us through humans as their host. Thomas began to prophesy to me and in his prophecy, he reveals to me this: You will be married at a young age, you will see your husband, but he will not see you, you will have three children, and you will be a prophetess.After the short revelation, my cousin found me to take me home. That concluded the time I had with the prophet Thomas.

I will conclude with a silent prayer that his works are guided by Christ and the Holy Spirit; may peace be with him where ever he may be.

8

The Truth:YOU MARRIED YOUR FATHER

I grew up watching my father battle the demons of addiction. I attribute the gift of compassion to his life. I was only eleven years old when my father woke me and my brother up from our sleep and pulled up a chair to tell us: *"I just want to tell you both this before anyone else has the chance to tell you."* My brother and I looked intently into our father's eyes, unaware of what he had to tell us. He looked back at us, without a flinch or breaking a sweat he said: *"I've been a heroin addict for over twenty years. I contracted HIV from sharing dirty needles."* I cannot in this moment at thirty-four years old tell this story without great pain in my heart and in my spirit.

That night was undoubtedly the worst night of mine and my brother's life. We sat there shaken by this devastating news, we cried our hearts out. That moment would change me forever. It taught me to live my life's truths, free from what others believed to be true about me, but in authenticity. On my thirteenth birthday, my dad came to my mom's house to bring me a birthday card. I was overjoyed that he was present, even though he spent most of the night shooting dope in the bathroom.

To the world he was a nobody, loser, and junky. Yet, he meant everything to me. That night of my birthday he gave me a card that was signed: *"Happy birthday, with unconditional love."* At thirteen years old I did not know what that meant. I later asked my mom: *"What is unconditional love"?* She replied: *"It means you love someone no matter what"* and I carried that in my heart from

29

that day forward and learned to love people, who I love, no matter what! I remember the bruised and battered body that had been used and abused by the demons that ravished his very existence, mentally, physically and spiritually. The power of these demons did not hide, they were loud, strong and bold.

I watched as they invaded his being and would not cease to give him rest. I knew that God could deliver my father and when his deliverance did not come, I wondered why. I needed to know what right demons had to take my father's life from him. I would often investigate the lives of people who were addicted to drugs, I could always feel a spiritual connection with them.I have always had a strong compassion and heartfelt desire to help them or try to feel their spirits.

Through that connection, I feel myself in their world, trapped, helpless, hopeless, afraid, lost, devastated, frightened, empty, abandoned, lifeless, desolate, broken, ashamed, wounded, ensnared, bound, shackled and in the grips of the devils embrace. I could look at them and see their lives as void. They were mere shells of something that used to exist but has long been dead to the new "thing" that has taken over them. It was like they were asleep in a faraway land while the demons that took a hold of them created new lives for them somewhere else. Controlling their movements, shaping their minds and leading them to a dark dungeon of evil tricks that would ultimately kill the person "who was asleep" for good, to gain total reign without worrying about that person ever coming back to claim their lives again. In time I would meet an old childhood trauma of mine head on.

9

The Truth:SEX DOES NOT HEAL SEXUAL ABUSE

I remember the skinny battered and bruised legs. The rips in my shirt, stains in my clothes, chipped nails and fog covering the skies. The brown bricks and empty lots. Overgrown grass and daisies. Hand prints in the dried cement. Scraped arms, bleeding hands. Tall shadows, funny grins, doorbells and buckets on strings. There were cherry sized drops of blood and humming birds. The earth stood still in a moments time and there were weary eyes and broken parts of me left behind. A sweet sound of mourning angels sang to me. There were paved roads ahead, with blinking lights, street signs and caved in rooftops. Broken down cars on curbs, over piled dumpsters with hungry dogs barking. *"There's a monster back there!"* was the echoing sounds of young girls before me who once treaded on that same broken road. Those old brown bricks hid remnants of saturated garments, missing barrettes, bows, ribbons and head ties. I remember seeing eyes wide shut staring out at me from the window panes. There were loud clanking sounds and thumps that came from the ground as my precious jewels fell from me. *Thump! Thump! Thump!* with every footstep.

The next step I took separated me from where I was. I found myself lost inside a maze of unfamiliarity. A world of uncertainties. *"I tried to look up high, yet my head hung low!"* I ran off into desolate places. I hid in the darkness of the night and buried myself in the wilderness of my palms. I bore dried fruits and the harvest reaped the regurgitated remains of little girls who were trapped, drowning and gasping for air. Their faces covered, eyes tightly closed, arms folded, tears streaming. They were kicking, screaming, frightened and alone *"Get your hands off me! Take your rope from around me!" Remove this duct tape, stop it, No! Go away!* Yet, no one knows. No one hears, no one sees! Hands continued to grope, remove, unbutton, unzip and uncover the treasures of their innocence. Running away with all their precious little things. *"Give them back!"* were the uttering sounds that spoke from the graves of many little girls lost and forgotten. Over the next two years I began to stay out in the streets, anywhere but home. My relationship with my mother was still on the rocks and she seemed not to care what I did, or where I was. I stayed out every night for as many nights as I pleased, wherever the wind would toss me. I was having sex on a regular basis with a boy from the neighborhood.I was naïve, and the streets exposed me to people and spirits that preyed upon young girls like me. I would sometimes go to see Joey at the crack house him and his cousins sold drugs out of. One night I slept there with him. After he had been drinking all night, he fell into a drunken stupor. I awoke from my sleep, early that morning, and was greeted by one of his friends who forcibly attempted to grab hold of me. I immediately started whaling on this guy.I was punching him with everything I had in me to let him know I was a fighter.

He punched me repeatedly in my face until I collapsed to the floor.Afterwards, he grabbed me and took me into the bathroom, where he bent me over and began to rape me. I thought about trying to get out of the bathroom and all I could envision was him bashing my head against the sink or tub. Ultimately, I did not escape my awful fate. One of the boys in the house opened the door and with a devilish grin upon his face, he stood there and watched as I was being brutally raped by this man, with tears streaming from my face and did not offer to help me.

Afterwards, my attacker walked me into the back bedroom and told me to sit down, I sat down with tears running down my face and he sat next to me and stuck his tongue out and asked me for a kiss. I told him no and he with more authority in his voice said: *"give me a kiss!"* After a few minutes of sitting there

I got up and ran to the front of the house where Joey was sleeping. I called his name attempting to wake him, but he lifted his head briefly and went back to sleep. I felt helpless and abandoned, and there was no one there to rescue me. The house was a two-family flat and we were upstairs on the second level of the flat. I thought about jumping from the balcony to escape but was again restrained by fear.After a while he allowed me to leave.

Once outside, I made my way up the street and headed towards my grand-mother's house, as she only lived around the corner from the crack house I was coming from. As I was walking, I could feel the presence of evil trapesing behind me. He came after me again slowly walking beside me all the while devising a plan to distract me with his empty apologies. By the time we got to the corner he had grabbed me again from behind, locking my arms and lifting me up from the ground.

I wore white pumpkin seeds that day and I can still remember the sound of the fluttering brush beneath my feet as he proceeded to drag me away, like that of a lion dragging its prey into the wilderness to devour. I can still remember the bright green grass stains on those pumpkin seeds and the thick dirt that covered them. I can still remember the smell of the fresh grass and the dreariness of the morning dew that produced wetness on the windows and the small drops of water that slowly rolled from them. Like that of tears falling from the heavens as the angels watched over me. My mind wondered: *Where have all the people gone? Who will come home? Who will leave out for work? Who will gaze out of their window?*

Suddenly, I was awakened with eyes wide opened as the birth of his relentlessness, pushed me out of my sub-conscience into the world of his vileness. After he got me half way to the entry point of the alley, he put his arm around my neck and the force of his grip compressed my air supply. My screams were faint, and they fizzled into the mist of the morning dew.I was silenced.

Through an alley behind a vacant building he forced me inside that brown, abandoned building with all the windows busted out. Once we got to the third floor of the abandoned building, he said: *"take your clothes off."* I stood there with tears streaming down my face, scared of what would happen to me next.

I shook my head no. I did not want to take my clothes off for him again. I did not want to smell the sourness that oozed from his pores like that of an alcoholic. I didn't want to be tainted by his pungent smell. I didn't want to taste the spit from his mouth as he kissed me. He again said, *"take them off or I am going to take them off for you!"* Again, here I stand thinking of a way to escape.

I wanted to jump from the third story window, right through the glass, but fear again had overcome me and my fate in that moment had made up its mind. He raped me again. After he finished, I walked back through the alley through the debris onto the sidewalk. I looked around and was in a daze from the brutal morning I endured. I was no longer held captive but was free. I walked down the street and an older gentleman driving down the road stopped and asked me if I was okay. I replied: *"No, I was raped."* The man offered me a ride to my aunt's house not too far from where I was, and he called the police and told them what happened. I was grateful for his help and concern. Satan ordered the attack and used my assailant to cause me both physical and psychological harm.

I felt defeated, outside of myself and exposed to the dark forces that had their way with me through this host I called my mother after she found out what happened from the police. *"What happened to you?* She asked. *"I was raped."* I replied. Her response was cold and not one you would expect from a mother whose only daughter was viciously attacked and raped. She says to me: *"You did not have any business over there!"* I was so angry, I could explode. I could not understand why she was not able to connect with me on a deeper more personal level. I wanted her to hold me in her arms and tell me that everything is going to be okay.I needed to hear her say: I am sorry that happened to you, are you ok? But nothing, she was cold as ice to me like she had always been. As cold as the winter months with ice sickles dripping from the gutters of a house. Nonetheless, I could not continue that phone conversation and be blamed for my attack.

I wanted to hear the sweet concerning voice of a mother that wanted to know her daughter was safe. I wanted her to tell me that I was loved and missed.Those are not the words I heard, and I slammed the phone down, in anger and disappointment. I did not want to hear that I was wrong or that I should have been at home. That moment in time would profoundly shape and mold the relationship, trust, respect and bond with my mother for years to come.

10

The Truth: YOU HAVE ANGER ISSUES

I was a problem child who got into many fights at school. I was overconfident and arrogant.I carried myself in a fearless way and anyone looking for trouble would find it. I was an adventurous child, who grew up with a lot of boy cousins. I had to be tough, and a fighter. I was in a series of fights, one in which led to me being kicked out of all Chicago public schools. It started with an altercation between my best friend Tanya, and a new girl that arrived at our school. Her name was Shannon. Shannon was pretty, with long curly hair and her mother dressed her in all the latest fashions that our parents could not afford. As you could imagine the rest of the girls were flat chested, had bad skin, were bald headed, and wore hand me down clothes from their siblings, cousins, and even wore clothes from their mother's wardrobe collection of old seventies and eighties party attire. The fight was fueled by jealousy and escalated into an all-out fight between students and parents. Shannon's mom arrived to pick her up from school that afternoon, only to find me and several of my classmates beating the girl to a pulp.

Shortly after, a special unit at the Chicago police department organized to combat gang activity in the community, arrived and took me and the other girls involved in the fight to the Juvenile detention facility. We were later released to the custody of our parents. Afterwards, Tanya's parents restricted all communication between me and her, as they believed I was a bad influence on their daughter. *"I was a bad influence?"* I thought. Tanya was the one who started the fight, and I jumped in to help her. We would later have to attend a court trial for the crime and was consequently, found guilty of assault with intent to cause great bodily harm-less than murder, and given probation. I went on to attend a preparatory school for girls on the North side of Chicago. I violated my probation for truancy, and I was never home when my probation officer would come by to visit. After the violation of my probation, I had to go back in front of the judge.

I was found guilty of truancy and awarded to the State of Illinois and would spend the next sixteen months of my young life incarcerated. I went from one group home to the next, until I was placed in my final group home. The girls who were already there, learned about my soon arrival, from the staff members.They knew I was violent with a bad reputation, so they showed respect to my crime. We were always made aware of the next girl's charges before they arrived, so that we could be ready to deal with anything that may have transpired. I met girls who like me were emotionally oppressed and suffered from psychological damage. We often had to restrain girls for acts of violence against other girls, and staff members. One of the girls would defecate in her room and smear feces all over the floors and walls and take the pumps from lotion bottles and stick them in her vagina to cause self-harm.

There was a girl who inserted a bobby pen in her arm before she came to the placement center and she would show us the pen in her arm moving around. Another was a girl who would scream in the middle of the night: Help me, the devil is after me, help me. I remember the staff members going inside of her room and carrying her out, and she cried and screamed *"The Devil keeps messing with me."* I have witnessed spiritual attacks on the minds of young girls that came to these facilities from different parts of the state. The system was bombarded with young girls who had been molested, raped and had parents who were drug addicted. Young girls who turned to prostitution to feed their own drug addictions.

A lot of these girls would be released only to return to the prison system years later, as adults. They are either serving life sentences or very lengthy prison terms For first and second-degree murder charges. I was on the fast track to self-destruction and could have easily ended up like any one of my peers. The lord's grace in my life is what has kept me throughout the years. Look at God, guiding me throughout the course of my youth. Placing me in the confines of youth homes to preserve my life!

11

The Truth: IT'S A THIN LINE BETWEEN LOVE & CODEPENDENCY

At the age of nineteen, I met my husband Howard who was eleven years older than me. Howard was self-sufficient, independent, intelligent and he was a natural born hustler who could turn nothing into something. Anything I needed he provided, and I adored him immensely. I was taken by the softness of his full lips that naturally puckered as we shared intimate kisses, his handsomely perfect structured face, with gorgeous features that were all aligned, chiseled and masterfully positioned to make him a sight for sore eyes, dark brown colored skin that could easily be mistaken as milk chocolate, tempting, enriching and delightful he was blessed with the gift of bringing out the best in me and my heart poured out broken pieces of me, before he came into my life:

There was a new part of me that was found. I had finally found someone who adored, cared and loved me. We had a connection that went beyond the physical likeness. We were connected spiritually. I would sometimes place my hand over his chest as he slept through the night to feel the rhythm of his heart. I could feel the intimate parts of him that wanted to be better. I connected with the pains of his life and could feel a great need in his life for something pure. My desire to be that for him was great.

There was nothing more real and beautiful to me in my life, until I met him.

Howard uncovered a hidden part of me that was designed only for him. There is undoubtedly, no other man in this world that could have ever nurtured the woman out of me, as he. Moreover; in great persistence, I stayed with him through every triumph, joy and pain.

Yet, there were deep rooted pains and insecurities that haunted me. It was in perfect order that we met each other and grew closer than friends and lovers. It would be an inseparable and unbreakable bond for years to come.

Though the years ahead would be faced with significant difficulties and challenges, it was the first time in my life, that I had experienced real love that was pure, beautiful, fulfilling, consistent, gratifying, and reciprocated. It was a love more powerful than any I have ever known, excluding none. I was caught by his charm, like that of a fish caught on a hook by an experienced fisher man. I was drawn to his gentleness, kindness, thoughtfulness, and benevolence and undoubtedly knew that God placed him in my path for a greater purpose that would someday be revealed to me. I had a vision that was given to me. In a vision I saw Howard and I sitting in a park enjoying the stillness on a hot summer day, sitting in lawn chairs on green grass that covered the entire park. It was brief and vivid.

It was a sure event that would one day soon be our reality. On one evening he visited me during our courtship, and I told him he would marry me, he was taken aback by the idea and was quite puzzled at the remark. For, we had only been in acquaintance for a short time. However; it was revealed to me and not to him.

Howard was everything I could ask for in a man, friend, lover, confidant and he would become my most trusted advisor. Though he was my great super hero, strong and mighty warrior of love that took my life and emotions by a raging storm, he was a weakened vessel of a man without power, and a victim to the lifestyle that he grew to blindly love. He lived his life at an accelerated pace that thrusted him into a whirlwind of corrupt and ill-gotten gains that would provide him the sense of false power, popularity, and fondness from loose women.

He had taken that lifestyle and mastered it, with precision and men who were in the same field as he, honed upon his skills. Even those who outwardly scorned and ridiculed him, secretly admired his abilities, as he was gifted in his trade. I always admired his uniqueness, and the many qualities he possessed that other men did not. Though his life was in the crossfire of the enemy's tricks, props, gimmicks and devices. I trusted God for him. I believed God for him. I carried him in my spirit, with great compassion and perfect anticipation to someday see the man that God would make over, heal, deliver and wash. He reminded me much of my father, a kind, passionate and gentle soul, but like my father he too battled with his own demons.

We became inseparable over the next few years and would later marry when I was twenty-three years old. Howard had a vicious cocaine habit, that would later develop into a full-fledged heroin addiction that mirrored the same devastating effects of my father's love affair with the goddess of heroin that users bowed to with sacrificial offerings, giving up to this dead idol all their gifts, children, homes, money, cars, clothes and most of all their souls. I watched helplessly as my husband undressed her, fondled her breasts and rested in the yoke of her bosom.

I would quietly weep, as he longed for her and only her. *My husband, whom I love and adore, when will you return to me? What is it about her love that has captivated your heart that I once held?* In retrospect, I recall moments that took me out of his company, to sustain the peace of mind I had left, and it forced me to insert small increments in time that would steal me from the madness of his obsession with his newly found love. My soul now reflects on those times, and I am still saddened by the emotional separation that divided us for a time.

The drugs caused a deep manifestation of demons and spirits to dwell within him and they enslaved him ferociously through mental and physical dependence. His daily routine was a "playground" built by the enemy as he would wander the streets of the city, chasing after his own calamity. Each corner had signs that pointed down dark treacherous roads that were setup as themes and plots. It was all laid out for him. Whatever pleasure, drug, defiled, and detestable thing. It was readily available to him.

Each road was planted differently. Some with great sink holes that would only appear if he went over them. Opening its mouth from the bed of the ground hoping to swallow him up. Another was filled with quicksand that would sink him deeper into the bowels of his own understanding. Nursing the birth of a mind that could not escape itself and he would become lost in all his ways. One road was made of great bodies of water that sought to drown out the voice of God that would speak to him throughout his life.

The other had fire that wanted to consume him. Others had wind that wanted to carry him away in violent and mighty storms that tossed him from one end of the earth to the next, as he went out searching and chasing after his next high. They were all methodically designed to ensnare him, and my heart cried out to God for him to be delivered from all the snares that the devil placed in his path as he ventured out into the wickedness of the world that hid its evilness behind the curtains of this life. Yet, all these things he could not see. Instead his eyes deceived him, and in his delusion, he ran blindly down roads that presented to him beautiful orchids that grew as tall and strong as trees. Paved streets of gold, waterfalls that dripped with sweetness, and fruits that bear true happiness, peace and wisdom if eaten.

They were all strategically planted devices, like that of land mines that soldiers use in the army to kill unsuspecting enemies that would place their feet behind enemy lines. This man that once was my protector and provider when I had no job, money or education; The man who taught me how to cook, drive, pay bills, dress, and raised me, began stealing money from me, pawning the TV's in the house, stealing from department stores, and anything he could think of to feed his God.

He became an expert at manipulation and a liar and demons would play tricks on him to taunt him.One night I lay in bed and watched through the doorway of our bedroom that was across from the bathroom. There he stood in the mirror after a three–day cocaine binge, with a small metal object in his hand, picking bugs out of his face that did not exist. He asked: "do you see the bugs going in and out of my pores?' I was swept into a place of deep sadness and I wept. This is the SCREAM, I'm talking about. These are the things that grip you! Insanity is a persistent knock at the door.

12

The Truth:YOU HAVE TO FIND YOUR VOICE

We moved into a small two-bedroom house, on the side of town my husband grew up. It was a fixer upper that one of Howard's friends owned. Half of the peach color siding had been ripped off by drug addicts that would sell the material for drug money. It was furnished with an old couch that was left there by the previous tenants. The flooring had hardwood floors that needed priming and still had the staples left in them from the carpet that was recently pulled up.There was a small space for a dining table, that I filled with a small glass table from the dollar store. It was a house, we dwelled in, but it was never made a home.

During those times we had heavy traffic at our house, because of my husband's lifestyle. He allowed different men to come in and out of the house, and even allowed a couple of them to live with us. I would walk through the door of my house, and on several occasions they would all be gathered in that small dining space around the glass table, and they would be either snorting cocaine or shooting heroin. Whatever their vices were, they had free reign to indulge.

One man I remember, snorted a line of cocaine and instantly he had demons jump on him, and he stood up frantically from his chair and looked at them and he shouted: "Get off me!" and my husband calmly told him it was okay and sit down.I stood in the background and thought to myself: *"Is this really my life?"* I knew the life and people I was subjected to was spiritually toxic. I heard demons at our window calling my husband's name early one morning. I can still feel the chill, and the hairs that stood up on the back of my neck from the sound of their voices, they were after him, they were trying to get his attention, they were calling his name repeatedly. It was a chilling encounter with the spiritual forces that lurk behind the scenes, going unnoticed, unseen, and unheard. I have heard the voices of demons before, but I thought they were gone.I put my face in the pillow and cried out to God, asking the lord what is happening to me?! Why is this happening to me?! I had snapped in a real and spiritual way, because of the demonic forces that surrounded me, they had created passageways through the heavy drug usage and the presence was fiercely strong. One night while I was asleep, I heard a female's voice coming from the living room, so I got up and walked in the room and there my husband sat on the couch in his underwear, with a girl standing over him.

I was a few seconds shy of catching him in the act of having oral sex performed on him, so of course he lied about it and said that nothing happened. Years later he confessed to me that she performed sexual acts for cocaine. Throughout the years he engaged in multiple affairs with women. I hated him, and myself for standing by his side through his addiction, jail, and multiple bouts of rehab that did not work.

I became embittered and resentful toward him, for the hell he brought into my life during those years. Years later, I would go on to have an adulterous affair with someone close to him, that sought to destroy the bond between us for his own reasons and personal vendetta. I was held captive in my desires and lust, my soul was not with me during those years. I allowed the devil to use me through chaos, confusion, division, sexual immortality and hate. My hate for my husband empowered me to stay in sin, and indulge in sexual endeavors that defiled my body, spirit, and marriage.

I engaged in sexual encounters with other women as well. I created a false desire to be with other women, to mask my insecurities. I was tricked into believing that I could somehow feel less insecure about more beautiful women if I slept with them. I wanted to be in control of my feelings. I had a spirit of perversion that kept me in bondage. I was unable to heal, and forgive, because I loved my hate. I welcomed it, I ate it for breakfast, lunch and dinner. I would not stop until I fed my need for revenge.

I wanted him to suffer for the multiple women he slept with throughout the years, and the drug abuse. Our marriage began to disintegrate and had become tainted with lies, adultery and betrayal. I flaunted the affair with this other man, in my husband's face. I wanted him to suffer and I was bold, and malicious. I exposed to my husband every sexual way I allowed this other man to use me through a late-night confession, which came by way of guilt that weighed heavily upon me.

Revenge was like the sweet taste of honey on my lips, I indulged and engorged my burning flesh with the sins of my adultery and all its desires. I walked deeper and deeper into the pits of hell, every time I allowed this other man to touch me, kiss me and penetrate me. I was a broken woman tricked by the enemy into bondage, A slave to my sin. I paraded around with the shame of my iniquities atop my head as if it were a royal crown! Shattered fragments of the woman God designed me to be were spread around the city streets, hotel rooms, parks, cars and dark rooms.

Late night rendezvous that hid the moans of a man's wife in the darkness of the night. Enslaved by the grips of a lover whose name was *Rah*, entangled in a web of continuous deceit. The lies dripped from my lips like that of honey from a honey comb.With each encounter the call of my God whispered my name, a sweet call of conviction for my soul to come out of adultery, to be washed of the filth, sweat, saliva, blood, mucous, and secretions that defiled God's temple and out of the pits of an adulterous affair I emerged from the belly of abominations, making a covenant with God never to return back to the vomit that spewed from the belly of my transgressions.

I was not lost in adultery by way of some "great lover" that captivated me. I was led astray by the evil desires of my heart that had long before him or any other person had already been birthed in me.There was a drastic change that had to be made in my inner being. I had to come to a place in my mind that would arrest my own will. I was physically free to do the things I wanted to do. Yet, I became restrained through the chastisement of the holy spirit. I had a vengeful spirit that sought to bring me to ruin and the trials of my life gave these evil spirits the gateway they needed to enter my life. They used my pains, trauma's and marital issues to control me and I did not resist.

I allowed them to use me as they pleased. The problem was the mere fact that I believed I could do whatever I wanted to do. I will tell you, that you will answer to the Almighty God, for all your sins. There is nothing that God does not know, hear or see. Oh, how my soul cried out to God to restore and rebuild my marriage from the ground up and as the Lord begin to purge the vileness of my iniquities from the bottom of my belly. The walls of defeat, division, rebellion, hostility, and bitterness came tumbling down, and we continue to grow in Christ and love.

It took the Lord to change me, for me to see the works manifest in my husband's life. Here I am, praying for his deliverance from the bondage of addiction. Yet, I am wretched in all my ways. We must be praying husbands and wives, if we want to see the works and blessings of God show up in our lives. We have a call to come into accountability and take responsibility for one another.

I had to release the woman the world made me and learn how to walk in the process of what God was doing and wanted to do in me and my husband's life. I am a witness that forgiveness is one of the best gifts you can give yourself and others. The weight of harboring other's trespasses will keep you bound to all kinds of demonic spirits. If you carry with you another person's sins, you will soon learn that the same spirits that birthed those sins, are still present, only now they have a new host.They are attached to the one who will not let them go. Do not prepare a house for demons to dwell! Remove the welcome mat for the devil and allow God to take rightful ownership.

13

Forsaking Yourself

There are key components that play significant roles in walking in the process of God's Purpose for our lives. In each one we identify God as the head. We identify God as the source. We identify God as having all power.

1. In this life we are living according to the will of God.
2. We do not define or create our own paths.
3. The process consists of many avenues.
4. We venture through darkness into the light of Christ.
5. We suffer for righteousness.
6. We are being internally made over to come into a great change.
7. We are called to do the work of God.
8. We are made uncomfortable in our circumstances.
9. People change, things change. (Provoking change in us.)
10. We have a desire for God.
11. We outgrow our former lives that were rooted in sin.
12. We experience the pains of leaving the old self behind.
13. We notice the gifts planted in us.
14. We surrender.
15. We cry out to God.
16. We have survived the birth pains of the conversion process through our

trials, heartache and sorrows. We develop into the purpose God created us for.

17.There is a need for redemption.

18.We begin to forgive others.

19.We are not ashamed of the past.

20.We rest upon his promises.

21.We testify to the works of Christ.

22.We praise God-In spite of.

23.We wait for God's direction.

24.We arrest our own will.

25.We crucify the flesh, little by little.

Throughout the course of my life, there are many pains, trials and tribulations I had to withstand. There were hills and valleys I had to get over. I lived here, I lived there.I worked, I was unemployed. I did not have money, I had money. I loved, I hated. I cried, and I laughed. I have had experiences that led me astray, and some that brought me back. Nonetheless, we must learn to walk in the process of what God's purpose for our life is. Do not be afraid of the process, the seasons do change.

We must go through some things to get to where we are going.We will go through some horrific, traumatizing and disheartening things. These are all processes that sustain us in obedience and teaches us that the spirit man is the precious jewel that is trapped inside the physical house of a man. The spirit man is crying, seeking and searching for it's great escape.

The flesh is greedy, selfish and perishable. Thus, we understand that we walk not in this life as full physical beings, but of spiritual beings. We are mere visitors in this earth for a short time. In wisdom we understand the transformation that will occur at the end. Thus, we live according to that truth.

For, we aimlessly wander in darkness, hoping to be brought into the light of God's goodness. In due season we began to understand the process that was essential to our growth in Christ. We learn to humble ourselves when the luxuries of this life know us no more. In faith we believe God for a greater remedy of things to come. Through the abundant mercies of the Almighty

God, we are effortlessly carried through the unseen traps of this life that are designed to imprison our minds, souls and bodies. Therefore, we rebuke the works of the enemy and confess with our mouths that Jesus is the one and only true living God- The Alpha and Omega.

This is not a time to be timid in that which we believe.There are forces that exist in this world hidden in places, people and things. We must seek God for understanding and knowledge. Therefore, we seek gifts to see and hear with spiritual eyes and ears. I am a witness to the truth and full gospel of Jesus Christ. Sometimes he must uproot old foundations, sometimes he must move you, sometimes he must provoke a change in your circumstances to use you according to his will. You may be someone in an extra-marital affair, God is calling you out of adultery.

The devil will create division in your household to drive separation between the two of you, who were made one flesh, through the sacred union of marriage. Thus, creating strife and hostility in that which was made beautiful through God. Protect your marriage and forgive everything with your whole heart.The lord never said it would be easy or perfect. He knows the areas in your life and in your marriage that needs to be restored, rebuilt and repaired. Surrender and submit to God in your marriage, and he will bless you abundantly. Believe that the God we serve is mighty and powerful.

He has dominion over all things, and he is a way maker! A source and guide when we need direction, peace and understanding If there is anyone struggling with old pain and resentment, it is time to heal and release people from any grudge you may be harboring.

This is a time of revival, God did not give us a spirit of rebellion and of hate. For the children of drug addicted parents, there is a great need of healing power that you must experience. I understand the deep manifestation of hurt, anger and resentment that has been planted in you. God is calling you to a place of forgiveness and peace. God is in position to deliver you from the pain and resentment. There is wonder working POWER in the name of Jesus! We come against the spirit of abandonment, uselessness and trauma. We have been uplifted to the presence of an almighty God who walks us through every rape, abandonment, addiction, mental collapse, trials and tragedy. Jesus is a

Balm in Gilead– A healer! Be free today from the past.

The Lord has released the grips of the enemy that has sought to enslave you through the sins of your mother or father. For we are walking through this life in a divine and heavenly purpose. With great compassion, encouragement and faith may we touch and agree that the yokes that bind the brokenhearted through old wounds be healed. In Jesus name we pray and believe. Amen

May God uplift you in whatever it is that you may need deliverance from. To the young girls suffering abuse, or under spiritual attacks of the mind. Fear not the things you may hear or see, for God is the creator of all things, and in him all things are held captive. Peace and blessings to you all.

II

Forgive

III

Deliverance

IV

Renewal

V

Hope

VI

Grace

VII

Mercy

VIII

Faith

IX

Long-Suffering

14

Conclusion

Finding Your Voice

In a world where life throws hidden snares, there are many women who parade behind the curtains of mass insecurities, sexual abuse, infidelity and a never-ending cycle of discontentment. "I Can't Love This Way" represents the very soul and nature of those women who long for the grandeur of things in faith, hope and the constant faces of strength. Mikiya Wilson gives an epic recount of events through trial, tragedy and triumph. "Colored By God: Black Girls Cry Too- A Black Girls Tale- With Poetic Prose" transforms the scenes of a woman's life into vivid words and journeys. To grow and develop into the woman you are created to be, you must first learn to find that inner voice that speaks out against anything in your life that has you bound. Often than not, that voice is not found until you have literally lost your mind!

Afterword

To find your voice is essential to self-discovery. I found myself in a series of unhealthy relationships, due to the suppressed voice that kept me in a constant cycle of abuse both physically and sexually. It wasn't until I faced the truth and reality of who I was. I did not like the person I had become. I had to reach some of the darkest times in my life to really come into the light. My voice was trampled by an abusive husband, lies and codependency. Once I tapped into that power that we all possess (the ability to hear God's voice.) only then was I able to speak up and against the things in my life that kept me silenced. I suffered for years, from low-self-esteem and low self-worth. It wasn't until I nearly went insane, that I was able to SCREAM my way out of the nightmare that imitated my life. I mean scream in both the literal sense and the spiritual sense that represents the moment of surrender giving all my troubles unto the lord. A desperate bolstering cry for deliverance from mental collapse and confusion. It is my greatest hope that you too, will find your voice and SCREAM your way out of the grips of oppression, anger and self-sabotaging behavior.

www.ingramcontent.com/pod-product-compliance
Lightning Source LLC
Chambersburg PA
CBHW072121150726
47999CB00005B/2064